SPORTS POSITIONS

HOCKEY: GOALIE

by Christina Earley

A Stingray Book

SEAHORSE PUBLISHING

Teaching Tips for Caregivers and Teachers:

This Hi-Lo book features high-interest subject matter that will appeal to all readers in intermediate and middle school grades. It may be enjoyed by students reading at or above grade level as well as by those who are looking for age-appropriate themes matched with a less challenging reading level. Hi-Lo books are ideal for ELL readers, too.

Each book appeals to a striving reader's age and maturity level. Opportunities are provided for students to read words they already know while encountering a limited number of new, high-interest vocabulary words. With these supports in place, students will read more fluently while increasing reading comprehension. Use the following suggestions to help students grow as readers.

- Encourage the student to read independently at home.
- Encourage the student to practice reading aloud.
- Encourage activities that require reading.
- Establish a regular reading time.
- Have the student write questions about what they read.

Teaching Tips for Teachers:

Before Reading

- Ask, "What do I know about this topic?"
- Ask, "What do I want to learn about this topic?"

During Reading

- Ask, "What is the author trying to teach me?"
- Ask, "How is this like something I already know?"

After Reading

- Discuss how the text features (headings, index, etc.) help with understanding the topic.
- Ask, "What interesting or fun fact did you learn?"

TABLE OF CONTENTS

WHAT IS A HOCKEY GOALIE?

Goalie or goaltender is a position on a hockey team.

Goalies stand in front of the net. They **prevent** the other team's shots from going into the net.

They have one of the most important positions on the ice. They are team leaders.

BAUER
cmbcasa
30
Reebok
Reebok
Reebok
Reebok
Reebok
HOCKEY MILANO

catching glove
sweater
padded pants
blocker

UNIFORM

Hockey goalies wear a jersey called a sweater.

They also wear padded goalie pants.

The catching glove is used to catch the puck. The blocker is a glove that holds a special hockey stick.

FUN FACT

Hockey goalies are prohibited from wearing number 0 or 00.

HELMET

Goalies wear a helmet or mask. It has a metal cage that protects the face.

Helmets cover the head and neck. Many are made of **fiberglass**.

Helmets help goalies feel safe even when they are making saves on their knees.

FUN FACT

Many professional hockey goalies wear helmets with special custom designs.

helmet

POLLEOsport
cashback
world
30
KLUB HOKEJA NA LEDU

BEFORE THE GAME

Hockey goalies train and practice.

On game day, they eat healthy meals and drink lots of water.

At the rink, goalies stretch and warm up.

They have teammates practice taking shots at them.

DURING THE GAME

Goalies stand in the goalie **crease** waiting to be shot on.

When a shot comes, goalies might get into a **butterfly position**. This helps them stop shots.

Goalies also help determine **icing penalties**.

FUN FACT

Only the goalie can be in the goalie crease.

butterfly position

Clint Benedict, 1923

HISTORY

The first NHL (National Hockey League) games were played in 1917. At that time, goalies were not allowed to dive for the puck. They did not wear any protective gear.

In the 1940s, goalies started wearing baseball gloves.

The first fiberglass face mask was used in 1959.

FUN FACT

Goalie Clint Benedict is credited for changing the rules.

TRAITS OF A GREAT HOCKEY GOALIE

Hockey goalies must stay calm under pressure.

They need **athleticism** to dive and make **acrobatic** saves.

Having **mental** toughness and learning from mistakes are also important.

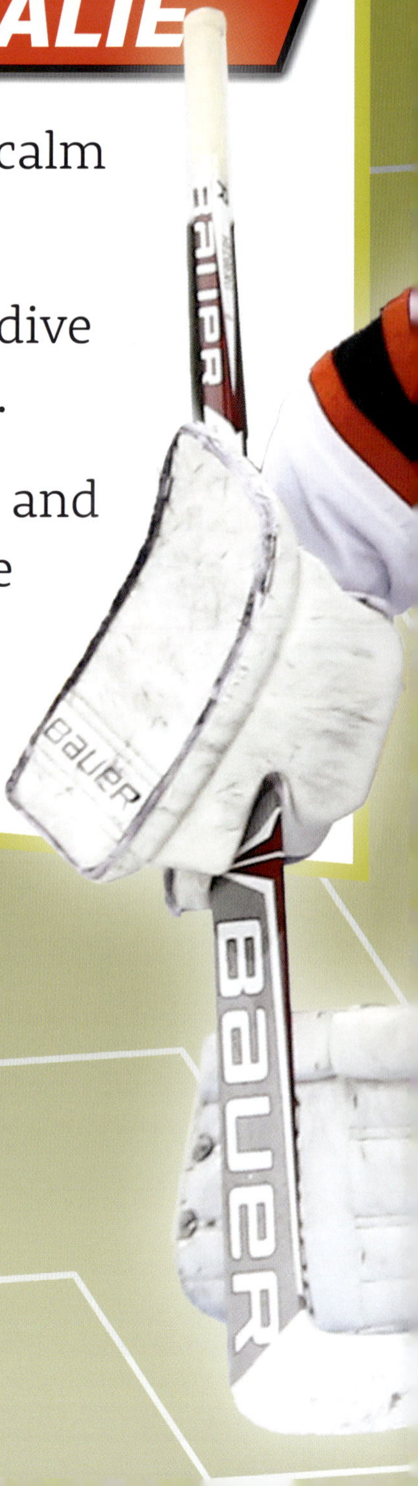

BAUER
BAUER

NOTES FROM THE COACH

- Be a leader on and off the field.
- Listen and take constructive criticism from coaches and teammates.
- Admit mistakes and improve.
- Have grit to never give up even when things are tough.
- Learn all parts of the game and all positions.
- Work hard during practices and in games.
- Eat a well-balanced diet.
- Have a good attitude and be respectful to others.

G.O.A.T. Greatest of All Time

JOHNNY BOWER

- Four-time Stanley Cup winner 1962, 1963, 1964, 1967
- Selected First NHL All-Star 1960–1961
- Vezina Trophy winner 1960–1961, 1964–1965

TURK BRODA

- Five-time Stanley Cup winner 1942, 1947, 1948, 1949, 1951
- Selected First NHL All-Star 1940–1941, 1947–1948
- Vezina Trophy winner 1940–1941, 1947–1948

MARTIN BRODEUR

- Three-time Stanley Cup winner 1995, 2000, 2003
- Selected First NHL All-Star three times
- Four-time Vezina Trophy winner

KEN DRYDEN

- Six-time Stanley Cup winner 1971, 1973, 1976, 1977, 1978, 1979
- Selected First NHL All-Star five times
- Five-time Vezina Trophy winner

GLENN HALL

- Stanley Cup winner 1961
- Selected First NHL All-Star seven times
- Three-time Vezina Trophy winner 1962–1963, 1966–1967, 1968–1969

DOMINIK HAŠEK

- Stanley Cup winner 2002, 2008
- Selected First NHL All-Star six times
- Six-time Vezina Trophy winner

JACQUES PLANTE

- Six-time Stanley Cup winner 1953, 1956, 1957, 1958, 1959, 1960
- Selected First NHL All-Star three times
- Seven-time Vezina Trophy winner

PATRICK ROY

- Four-time Stanley Cup winner 1986, 1993, 1996, 2001
- Selected First NHL All-Star four times
- Three-time Vezina Trophy winner 1988–1989, 1989–1990, 1991–1992

TERRY SAWCHUK

- Four-time Stanley Cup winner 1952, 1954, 1955, 1967
- Selected First NHL All-Star three times
- Four-time Vezina Trophy winner

GEORGES VEZINA

- Stanley Cup winner 1916, 1924
- Seven-time NHL Games Played leader
- Vezina Trophy for Best NHL Goalie named after him

GLOSSARY

acrobatic (ak·ruh·BAT·ik): like an acrobat; performed with leaping and other gymnastic feats requiring skillful control of the body

athleticism (ath·LE·tuh·si·zuhm): athletic ability; having the speed, strength, and agility of an athlete

butterfly position (BUHT·ur·flye puh·ZISH·uhn): dropping your knees and knee pads to the ice with your legs spread in opposite directions

crease (krees): the shaded area in front of the goal; the zone where the goalie makes saves and where opposing players are not allowed to interfere with the goalie

fiberglass (FYE·bur·glas): a strong material made from very fine glass fibers

icing penalties (EYE·sing PEN·uhl·teez): team punishments for breaking the rules and shooting a puck from your team's half of the ice over the opposing team's red goal line

mental (MEN·tuhl): of the mind

prevent (pri·VENT): to keep something from happening; to stop

INDEX

AFTER READING QUESTIONS

1. What protective equipment do hockey goalies wear?
2. Who can enter the crease?
3. What is a blocker?

About the Author

Christina Earley lives in sunny Florida with her husband and son. She has always loved different sports. She enjoys traveling to see different stadiums, arenas, and ballparks where she always has to eat the local hot dog.

Written by: Christina Earley
Design by: Kathy Walsh
Editor: Kim Thompson

Photographs/Shutterstock: Cover, p 3Jai Agnish, Adam Vilimek, Express Vectors; p 3-22 Express Vestors; p 5, 6, 9, 10, 13, 14, 17, 18, Adam Vilimek; p 5 BrunoRosa; p 6 Pavel L Photo and Video; p 9 Luca Santilli; p 10 DarioZg; p 13 Robert Nyholm; p 14 @Wiki; p 17 Debby Wong; p 18 nmphoto; p 23 kapona

Library of Congress PCN Data
Hockey: Goalie / Christina Earley
Sports Positions
ISBN 978-1-6389-7982-1 (hard cover)
ISBN 979-8-8873-5041-7 (paperback)
ISBN 979-8-8873-5100-1 (EPUB)
ISBN 979-8-8873-5159-9 (eBook)
Library of Congress Control Number: 2022941998

Printed in the United States of America.

Seahorse Publishing Company
www.seahorsepub.com

Published in the United States
Seahorse Publishing
PO Box 771325
Coral Springs, FL 33077

SEAHORSE PUBLISHING